the way to tea

YOUR ADVENTURE GUIDE TO SAN FRANCISCO TEA CULTURE

www.waytotea.com
Book concept and creation by Jennifer Leigh Sauer
The Way to Tea © 2007 Jennifer Leigh Sauer
Text © 2007 Jennifer Leigh Sauer
All Photographs © 2007 Jennifer Leigh Sauer
Cover Design ©2007 Jennifer Leigh Sauer
ISBN-13: 978-1-60109-009-6

Foreword by James Norwood Pratt
Way To Tea Calligraphy by Winnie Yu, Teance

The information in this book has been checked for accuracy and is correct to the best knowledge of the author. This volume is meant to offer the reader only a portion of the vast information available about tea. The reader alone is responsible for the use of any ideas or information provided by this book, and the author disclaims all liability in connection with the use of this information.

Printed in China by Palace Press

EARTH AWARE

Earth Aware Editions
17 Paul Drive
San Rafael, CA 94903
415.526.1370
www.earthawareeditions.com

YOUR ADVENTURE GUIDE TO SAN FRANCISCO TEA CULTURE

the way to tea

by jennifer leigh sauer

EARTH AWARE

tea

te

茶

thee

thé

ja

çaj

shaax

چای

thea

Chá

FOREWORD · 8

INTRODUCTION · 10

TEA BEFORE, A LITTLE TEA LORE · 16

RED BLOSSOM TEA COMPANY · 22

SAMOVAR TEA LOUNGE · 26

IMPERIAL TEA COURT · 32

JAPANESE TEA GARDEN · 36

RITZ CARLTON · 40

URASENKE FOUNDATION · 44

TEA GARDEN SPRINGS · 52

FAR LEAVES TEA · 56

TEANCE · 60

POLENG LOUNGE · 64

GREEN GULCH ZEN CENTER · 68

TAL·Y·TARA POLO & TEA SHOPPE · 72

SECRET GARDEN TEA HOUSE · 80

LELAND TEA COMPANY · 84

MODERN TEA · 88

DYNASTEA · 92

LOVEJOY'S ANTIQUES & TEA ROOM · 96

VITAL TEALEAF · 102

A FEW THOUGHTS FOR THE POT · 106

TEA: THE INSIDE SCOOP · 108

BASIC TEA GLOSSARY · 113

TEA FOR HEALTH AND VITALITY · 122

SUGGESTED READING · 124

ACKNOWLEDGMENTS · 126

venues

FOREWORD

James Norwood Pratt
Author, *The Tea Lover's Treasury*
www.teasociety.org

EVERYBODY WHO LOVES TEA OR loves San Francisco is sure to love this book. Like China's legendary emperor, Shen Nung, Jennifer Sauer discovered tea by accident. This accomplished photographer and woman-of-the-world was ambling through San Francisco's Chinatown and POW! She had the great fortune of stumbling upon tea's bright world of textures, hues, fragrances, flavors, exotic names and — best of all — the amazing "tea people" who helped chart her path through the Bay Area tea scene.

The sister- and brotherhood of tea drinkers, dating back about 5,000 years, is arguably the oldest social grouping on the planet that anybody can join. People have been getting together to drink tea and talk since the pyramids were under construction. When their talk turns to tea itself, there are historic and economic, medicinal, artisanal and even spiritual aspects to discuss. This conversation had been going on in Asia for 4,000 years or so before the first Europeans began drinking tea a mere 400 years ago, and joined the discussion.

Today Americans are recovering from a long national deprivation of tea — not teabag tea but the genuine article. Not all teabags are contemptible (to be fair), but most are beneath contempt (to be honest), and these lowered our parents' tea expectations. They came to expect a plain brown beverage with practically no variation from brand to identically packaged, identically priced brand. They forgot the very names of teas invoked by poets a generation earlier — "congou, hyson, bohea and a few lesser divinities" — and forgot that the world of tea, like the world of wine, is infinitely various and filled with infinite delights, each in its fresh particularity of difference.

San Francisco seems to have been the first place in America to rediscover these eternal truths. To quote what I wrote years ago introducing a tea book of my own, "… anyone writing a book about tea is wise to live in San Francisco, where friends from around the world may be discovered living next door. It is hard to imagine anywhere else that somebody from the North Carolina countryside might be made Honorary Director of the first traditional Chinese teahouse in the Western Hemisphere, but that is exactly what happened to me."

You hold in your hands Jennifer Sauer's account of exactly what has aroused and awakened in her as she was welcomed into the most eclectic, exciting and profoundly rich tea culture in the world: American tea culture, originating here in San Francisco.

Everywhere else in the world there's a "traditional" way to enjoy tea. The English like their Afternoon Tea just so, while the Japanese ceremony offers very different pleasures, and the Chinese — well, you get the idea. Jennifer shows us that all these tea traditions are alive and open to newcomers here by the San Francisco Bay. We are America's NEW tea lovers, heirs to all the tea traditions of the world.

~James Norwood Pratt, February 2007

One of the world's leading authorities on tea and tea lore, James Norwood Pratt is the author of the classic work, The Tea Lover's Treasury. *He lives in San Francisco.*

introduction

IN CHINA ABOUT FIVE THOUSAND years ago, some leaves from an overhanging tea tree blew into the pot of boiling water of Emperor Shen Nung as he was about to cook a meal in his garden. He was a scholar and master herbalist, and reputedly possessed superhuman powers including a transparent stomach through which he was able to see and analyze the effects of medicinal plants. As he drank his first cup of tea, he could see the infusion drawing poisons out of his intestines, and he knew he had come upon a highly medicinal plant that deserved attention and reverence.

Like Shen Nung, I too accidentally "discovered" tea while on a mission to make some colorful photographs for a client. My circuitous and unanticipated adventure — from Chinese teahouse to Japanese garden to British salon — also led to a revelation that San Francisco is uniquely situated at the epicenter of an exploding American tea culture, replete with myriad expressions and manifestations of tea, from the whimsical and gregarious to the subtle and austere.

One afternoon, I had packed up my cameras and ambled down San Francisco's Grant Street to explore the vibrant world of Chinatown. I was soon beckoned into a tea-tasting shop sprinkled with people chatting and sipping premium teas. Textures and colors softly surrounded me in a kaleidoscopic whirl. Bright tins containing teas with names such as "Iron Goddess of Mercy" and "Bitter Dragon Ball" captured my imagination and my eye. Gorgeous leaves of all shapes, hues, and fragrances filled large glass jars on the wall, and customers' faces lit up with awe as bulbs of tea plunged into wine glasses of steaming water exploded into lovely flowers before their eyes. Pure Nirvana for any photographer — or tea lover.

opening

approach

preamble

proem

lead

debut

Best, of all, I found myself surrounded by an uncannily interesting group of people from many parts of the world, all laughing and talking about art, culture, love and — most of all — tea. Some talked about its medicinal benefits; others related tales of tea's economic and spiritual impact on different continents; still others spoke of how to pair teas with foods, and of the fragrances and bouquets wafting from the small steaming porcelain cups.

Uncle Gee, the proprietor of this tea-tasting shop, said it best: "Tea culture is not only about tea. It's about purifying your body and your soul. We are here to benefit people, to offer tea as medicine for the body and the mind, and to give people a place to share their life stories and ideas." In short, tearooms provide something life-affirming and valuable to the community, just as they have for thousands of years. Teahouses in China still serve as gathering places for making business deals and sharing gossip; Japanese tearooms invite meditation, mind cleansing, and reflection; and English salons offer refinement, repose, and connection. All offer a gracious respite from banality and daily routine.

As I began to study the five-thousand-year history of tea, I realized that regardless of the culture it impacts, tea gathers people together and draws out the best in them. Indigenous healers might even consider the tea plant, *Camellia sinensis*, to be a "master plant" for its ability to heal so many different peo-

ple and cultures in so many varied ways. In fact, natural healers, scholars and Buddhist monks were responsible for introducing tea from one continent to another, as it developed a reputation for stimulating the mind and the senses while also inviting repose, reflection and relaxation.

Each time tea is introduced to a new land, it evolves and mutates into a new "tea culture" that profoundly influences that society — socially, spiritually and economically. Because of the stunting effects of the Boston Tea Party, in which pre-Revolutionary Americans snubbed their noses at English taxes and tea, the United States is only now belatedly developing a tea culture, and the San Francisco Bay Area is the polestar of this event. As the most diverse, sophisticated, eccentric, open-minded and creative urban center in the world, only the San Francisco Bay Area could usher in the new American tea culture.

The region is blessed with a profusion of contrasting tea traditions from which to draw. In no other place and at no other time could there emerge such an eclectic, exciting and multifarious tea scene. Chinese, Japanese and British customs all play strong roles, as they mingle and fuse with the sometimes sophisticated and sometimes "funkadelic" ambience for which the Bay Area is so well known. Tea takes on many expressions and attitudes here, and we can lavish in its elegance, whimsy, exoticism or austerity, as the mood moves us.

A person could spend a lifetime pursuing the art of tea and still have only a modest grasp of its immeasurable facets and manifestations. This is what makes tea so engaging and "tea people" so distinctly humble and also diverse in their vision of tea. Our "tea people" — those proprietors and teachers at tea shops, tearooms, tea foundations, tea lounges and tea nightclubs — are worth knowing and talking to. They come from all over, and each offers a different piece of the San Francisco tea puzzle.

The Bay Area is home to some of the most profoundly knowledgeable tea experts on the planet, from Roy Fong at Imperial Tea Court, America's oldest traditional Chinese teahouse, to Dynastea's May Hung, a descendent of Confucius as well as a licensed Chinese national tea examiner, to Alice Cravens, formerly the tea maven at Chez Panisse and now the proud owner of Modern Tea, to Urasenke Foundation's Christy Bartlett, to whom people travel from Japan in order to study Japanese tea ceremony.

Truly, the list goes on, as you will read in these pages. You could not find such a concentration of divergently focused tea professionals anywhere else in the world, and this only enhances the experiences and opportunities available to tea lovers and aficionados who live here or visit to explore the marvels of our blossoming tea culture.

This book is a starting point and by no means a complete reference to the dozens of tea shops, tea lounges and educational forums for all things *Camellia sinensis* in and around San Francisco. Nor is it the first and last academic word on tea. It is your invitation to America's new tea culture, which is brewing at its aromatic best in the Bay Area.

Primary tea venues were chosen with a handful of criteria. First, the location had to have tea as its primary focus. Second, a different aspect of San Francisco tea culture had to be conveyed by each spot to avoid redundancy. And third, the site had to present the values I have come to associate with tea: to provide intimacy and sanctuary from routine and banality; to encourage social engagement and the sharing of knowledge, friendship and spirit; and to offer heightened stimulation of the senses. In other words, each had to be intimate, unique, engaging, relaxing, and delightful.

So, I cordially offer you this invitation to our local tea party, whether a Chinese tea tasting event, an afternoon tea at a luxury hotel, an austere Japanese tea ceremony, or a night out with friends at a tea nightclub. You can bring a hat, a kimono, a fan, a bird, a book, or a pair of white gloves. Or just come as you are. You'll fit right in. I promise.

~ Jennifer Leigh Sauer, February 2007

the way to tea

tea before,
a little tea lore

TEA'S ACCIDENTAL DISCOVERY REPLAYS itself over and over as more and more people become aware of its power not only to heal the body, mind and spirit of the individual, but to mend and attenuate the ills of society as well. Its relevance as a catalyst to community, relaxation, harmony — and the stillness that provides for the engagement of conscience and integrity — is in evidence in the cultures that have embraced it, and in some cases, literally bowed to it.

Tea culture's long history, dating back well before the emergence of Christianity, is steeped in spiritual, philosophical, political and artistic traditions. It has been the impetus of poetry, meditation, civil disobedience and all-out war. Tea's value as a medicine and object of ritual was transmitted from one village or country to another almost exclusively by scholarly letters, books and documents or through oral discourse by religious priests, which greatly enhanced its mystery and reputation.

In 780 AD, the Taoist scholar Lu Yu wrote the first Chinese book about tea, *Ch'a Ching (The Classic of Tea)*, which specified ancient practices and rituals relating to tea cultivation and preparation. Over time, tea culture even influenced the political and economic landscape of many countries, creating demand for various teas and utensils used for preparation, consumption and ceremony, and also recasting social rules of exchange between political and religious dignitaries.

The Chinese began gathering in special teahouses to share gossip and make business deals long before English "high tea" came to be. Over the centuries, tea drinking in China became a social and spiritual endeavor, gaining favor in every stratum of society from imperial courts to rural teahouses. As tea made its journey to new continents, it consistently debuted as a medicine, gaining favor in high society and then becoming popular with the peasant and working classes.

For nearly four thousand years, the Chinese kept tea all to themselves. It was first brought to Japan from China as medicine by Buddhist priests during the T'ang Dynasty (618-907 AD), and grew to become ritualized by the Zen monks for whom the art of tea provided grist for meditation and ceremony. The highly choreographed Japanese tea ceremony soon developed into a social attraction for the elite Samurai society, and the very specialized ritual continues today to pay homage to its historical roots. Still lauded for its medicinal benefits, Japanese green tea is not only Japan's "national beverage," but is used in every food imaginable, from rice crackers to ice cream.

It wasn't until the late 1500s to early 1600s that tea started moving beyond the Orient to Russia via the Silk Road, and later to Central Asia, the Middle East and Europe. Europeans first heard about tea from Portuguese Catholic evangelists in China who wrote home about tea's great taste and medicinal value. The Dutch East India Company later paired with the Portuguese to monopolize the intercontinental spice and tea trade. Originally thought to be strictly medicinal and perhaps even an antidote to plague, tea evolved into a fashionable libation for the very rich in the Netherlands, who alone could afford the hundred-dollar-per-pound price tag. The Hague soon became the epicenter of European tea culture, and soon after that, in the mid- to late seventeenth century, tea became the beverage in vogue for English royalty whose fashions and fads were, as always, quickly embraced by English society.

Around the same time that Charles II's famed Portuguese tea-loving bride, Catherine of Braganza, was sipping her cuppa in the old country, tea made its first appearance in pre-revolutionary America through the Dutch settlers in New Amsterdam (now known as New York), who arrived as avid tea drinkers from Europe, and in fact, outnumbered all the tea drinkers in England. As tea was heavily taxed, a black market tea enterprise developed among colonists who snubbed the East India Company's very expensive imports, sparking the historical Boston Tea Party. "Take your tea and shove off," was the message from those who dressed in costume as Indians and with tomahawks broke open and threw overboard three shiploads of tea chests in defiance of the Crown and her duty-laden tea. So, as it turned out, tea was pivotal in provoking the American Revolution.

The rest was not only history but also became our present and future. Fast forward a couple of hundred years to contemporary America, and you will find a tea culture newly in the making. Had we

not told the British that they weren't our cup of tea, we might be sipping only English Breakfast and Earl Grey. Instead, our belated fascination with tea is inspired as much by the later-migrating Asian traditions and influences as it is by those of the Occident. Stimulated by the many cultures in the Bay Area which merge, blend and mingle so beautifully, we are building a marvelous alchemical tea culture that is unmatched and unrepeatable anywhere else in the world. You can enjoy Japanese tea ceremony at a mountainside Zen retreat in the morning and High Tea at a luxury urban hotel in the afternoon. Being true to our own slightly rebellious and provocative collective identity, we will even defy all tradition and go to a tea nightclub for a mixed drink with green tea at midnight. Regardless, Ducky, we will have our tea as we please.

venues | **PART ONE**

RED BLOSSOM

SAMOVAR TEA LOUNGE

IMPERIAL TEA COURT

JAPANESE TEA GARDEN

RITZ CARLTON

URASENKE

RED BLOSSOM TEA COMPANY

831 Grant Avenue
San Francisco, Ca 94108
415.395.0868
www.redblossomtea.com
Hours: Mon – Sat, 10 a.m. to
6:30 p.m; Sun, 10 a.m. to 6 p.m.

IF YOU KNOW NOTHING ABOUT TEA when you arrive at Red Blossom Tea Company, you will feel like a wizard when you leave. Few places offer so much information about so many different quality teas. This family-owned business is a centerpiece of San Francisco tea culture, and after more than a quarter century of doing business in Chinatown, customers keep coming back for more. You can trust their long tenure as an unsurpassed purveyor of premium teas and artisan teaware, yet you will not be met with haughtiness when you enter this elegant shop.

When the lids come off the large tea cans, the shop becomes suffused with their fragrances, and your every nerve will kneel to the music of their very fine teas, most of which are directly sourced from growers. Along with immaculate standards for traditional Chinese teas comes a great joy and intellectual vigor for

discussing and tasting tea. The ever-so-hip and sophisticated co-owner, Peter Luong, will riff on pu-erhs and oolongs like a jazz musician on a piano. His sister, Alice Luong, is also quite charming and extremely knowledgeable, and will pour you several cups of the most delicious teas while relaying the details of their origins and the methods by which they were processed.

This is a place to get anyone of any age excited about tea or to refine your tea palate and knowledge. If you don't have a chance to get to Chinatown, you can still order teas, teapots and *gaiwans* (brewing/sipping cups) on their excellent and easily navigable website.

urbane   steel and glass

yerba buena

eclectic

SAMOVAR TEA LOUNGE

Yerba Buena Gardens Location:
730 Howard Street
San Francisco, Ca 94103
415.227.9400
www.samovartea.com
Hours: Daily, 10 a.m. to 8 p.m.

Castro Location:
498 Sanchez Street
San Francisco, Ca 94114
415.626.4700
www.samovartea.com
Hours: Daily, 10 a.m. to 10 p.m.

DESPITE ITS VERY CONVENIENT, central location in Yerba Buena Gardens, the Samovar Tea Lounge is nearly invisible until you walk up the steps beside the waterfall to the upper terrace garden. When you find it, you will not forget it. This gorgeous glass and steel building provides a great view out to the garden and puts you in the catbird seat for taking in the ambience of San Francisco's chic arts district.

This stunning yet relaxing urban oasis is matched by its inimitable menu. Samovar struck me as being the most eclectic contemporary tea venue in San Francisco, offering American, Chinese, English, Russian, Indian, Japanese and Moorish tea services. Each comes with a cup of tea and a full meal — including dessert. As well, you will be served with teaware imbued with the feeling of that same culture.

While Samovar is serious about tea, they don't take themselves too seriously. If you order the American tea service, for example, this will likely be the first time you will encounter a bison burger on a crumpet. Pair that with iced tea, potato salad and trail mix, and you've got a meal you can get Uncle Bob or the kids to eat while you, perhaps, explore the more exotic Moorish mint green tea with grilled *halloumi* goat cheese kebabs, *dolmas*, olives and dates stuffed with *chèvre*. If you just want to learn a little more about tea, look for owner Jesse Jacobs, who offers wise and heartfelt discussions on teas at the earthy tea-tasting bar. No great trip to San Francisco would omit a visit to the Samovar Tea Lounge. You will wish they offered sleepovers.

IMPERIAL
TEA COURT

Original Chinatown Location:
1411 Powell Street
San Francisco, Ca 94133
800.567.5898 | 415.788.6080
www.imperialtea.com
Hours: Daily, 11 a.m. to 6:30
p.m. (Closed Tues)

Ferry Building Location:
1 Ferry Building Plaza
San Francisco, Ca 94111
415.544.9830
Hours: Sat – Wed, 10 a.m. to
6 p.m.; Thur – Fri, 10 a.m.
to 7 p.m. (Closed Mon)

IF SAN FRANCISCO HAD A PATRON SAINT OF TEA, it would be Roy Fong, owner of Imperial Tea Court, the country's longest running traditional Chinese tearoom. Now with two new locations, one in SF's Ferry Building and one in Berkeley, the Imperial is expanding with the Bay Area's exploding enthusiasm for tea. Roy Fong knows his teas, if anyone does, which is clearly in evidence by the inventory in stock. He is loved and respected by all who know him and works hard to make sure his part of San Francisco tea culture is held to the highest standard.

Imperial Tea Court offers *Gong Fu Cha,* or formal Chinese tea presentation, in Yixing clay teapots, which are made from a special purple clay found only in Yixing China. This classic way of preparing tea is considered a great art in China, and the expertise of the tea server is usually judged by how well he or she can brew

chirp

Yixing

root

community

tradition

three cups of different tasting tea from one serving of tea leaves. People spend lifetimes practicing and refining this age-old art.

The original Imperial Tea Court in Chinatown has the feel of an old Chinese tearoom and is a community hub for spirited lovers of art, culture and tea. The tearoom attracts regulars as well as tourists and those recently enchanted by tea. As a special touch, yellow chortling birds hang in lovely Chinese birdcages as icons of a not-so-distant time when local bird lovers would take their birds "for a stroll" to the Imperial, and then compare notes on the beauty of each one's unique song and the one-of-a-kind, handmade cages they inhabited, all the while sipping tea. You will hear many languages in this international environment, but in the end, all tongues speak of tea.

imperial tea court

maples

reflections

nippon

koi

JAPANESE TEA GARDEN

Tea Garden Drive | Golden Gate Park
San Francisco, Ca 94118
415.752.1171
www.sfgov.org/site/recpark_index.asp
Hours: Daily, 9 a.m. to 4:45 p.m.

THE JAPANESE TEA GARDEN is one of San Francisco's oldest treasures. A mosey through the five-acre garden eventually brings you to a Japanese style teahouse, which is more about the fun of sipping tea in America's oldest public Japanese garden than it is about understanding Japanese tea culture.

This unique garden, which was originally a one-acre exhibition for the 1894 World's Fair in San Francisco, slowly grew into a mature, larger garden. Many objects and structures in the park have been donated to the City over the years, including the 9,000-pound Lantern of Peace presented by the children of Japan. The garden has evolved over the years, and many structures have been renovated, including the teahouse, which was reconstructed and remodeled in 1959. This enduring tea garden features unique bridges, bronze sculptures, ponds and a wide assortment of Japanese trees and plants. You won't want to miss the large bronze Buddha, which is more than 200 years old and seems to offer the smile of the ancients.

The teahouse holds a good number of people, so even if you arrive on a sunny Sunday afternoon, you shouldn't have to wait for a table. This open-air building looks out over an elevated waterfall and fish-filled koi pond. The teahouse serves several kinds of teas in small Japanese style teapots and also offers crackers and fortune cookies. Incidentally, America tasted its first fortune cookies here, as the aphorism-filled wafers were introduced to the U.S. by the garden's creator and caretaker, Makoto Hagiwara. This is a wonderful place to stroll, dream or enjoy a cup of tea with a special friend.

RITZ CARLTON

Lobby Lounge: 600 Stockton Street
San Francisco, Ca 94108 | 415.296.7465
www.ritzcarlton.com/hotels/san_francisco
Hours: Mon – Thurs, 3:30 to 4:30 p.m.;
Fri, 2:30 to 4:30 p.m.; Sat & Sun, 1 to 4:30 p.m.

YOU WILL BE ADRIFT IN LEMON CURD and clouds of clotted cream. If you weren't imbibing during the most elegant afternoon tea in San Francisco, you would raise the cup of lemon curd to your lips and lick it clean. Well, maybe no one's looking ...

But they are. After all, this is the *Ritz*, the place to see and, worse (in this case), to be seen. The harp music will make you feel like you are on a proverbial heavenly cloud, being watched over by the spirits of society women who look out from the elegant paintings and tapestries that hang like angels by the silk brocade draperies and just beneath the crystal chandeliers. The clean, white linen will help you to recover from the ravages of the real world. Only the bill might bring you back to earth.

Actually, you will get far more than you pay for, guaranteed. The luxury is so stunningly beautiful, you would be hard-pressed to find a detail to mend; even the well-heeled clientele bring barely a wrinkle around the eye to the table. Chalk it up to all that healthy, age-defying, antioxidant-laden tea they are drinking.

elegance

white gloves

savoir-vivre

polish

Four kinds of tea service are offered here: Traditional, Royal, Premier and Vegetarian. You may also order teas or menu items a la carte. Tea towers feature fruit, scones, absolutely divine finger sandwiches, English teacakes and pastries. The Ritz offers an impressive selection of twenty teas, including Earl Grey, Lapsang Souchong, Japanese green teas and several herbal infusions. Champagne is also served. This is a fine place for a bridal shower, birthday celebration or to impress an important date or client.

tranquility

respect

purity

harmony

the way to tea

URASENKE FOUNDATION

2143 Powell Street | San Francisco, Ca 94133
415.433.6553 | www.urasenke.org
Hours: Monthly open-hearth tea gatherings;
check website or call for a schedule of classes

IF EVER YOU HAD A YEN to learn Japanese tea ceremony, you should know how fortunate you are to have a master *sensei* in your own backyard. American Christy Bartlett was personally assigned by the Urasenke Head Tea Master in Kyoto — with whom she had studied — to form the San Francisco branch of the Urasenke Foundation, which is a forum for educational and aesthetic experience with Japanese tea ceremony.

This is not a casual tea shop, so don't pop in for an unscheduled cup of tea. This is a place for perfect manners, while at the same time you may see students laughing with pleasure during this highly choreographed preparation of powdered green tea. There is a way to touch and direct each object, a way to sit, a way to speak and a way to sip. This is the way of tea.

The kindness and consideration that graze the formality of Japanese tea ceremony are mirrored by the soft brushstrokes skimming the long paper scrolls in this most austere and serene tea room.

"Pure wind sweeps the bright moon. The bright moon sweeps the pure wind," reads the scroll. Examining the bowl from which he had just sipped his freshly whisked tea, the guest at Urasenke is encouraged by his teacher to delicately question the host. He must politely seek information from her, which contributes to the harmony of the ceremony. "Your bowl is like a bright moon, Keiko. Please tell me more about it," he says.

Finally, it's a secret pleasure to learn that you can put the bowl right up to your face with both hands, tilt your head back and drink as much green tea as you please in one gulp or more. (I wish we could do this with the little cups of lemon curd at the Ritz.)

venues | **PART TWO**

TEA GARDEN SPRINGS

FAR LEAVES

TEANCE

POLENG

GREEN GULCH

TAL-Y-TARA

TEA GARDEN SPRINGS

38 Miller Avenue | Mill Valley, Ca 94941
415.389.7123
www.teagardensprings.com
Hours: Mon – Sat, 9:30 a.m. to 7:30 p.m.;
Sun, 10:30 a.m. to 7:30 p.m.

IN THE HEART OF MILL VALLEY, just North of the Golden Gate Bridge, you will find Tea Garden Springs, a holistic health spa that offers a novel indoor tea garden replete with a rock- and rose-strewn stream. At Tea Garden Springs, Tao meets Zen meets nineteenth century Europe. The walls are graced by the enchanting murals of Linn May, depicting scenes from Asian and Occidental tea gardens. Original Buddhism-inspired paintings by Kimberly Howland pay homage to the origins of Asian tea culture.

Some people come for soothing, re-energizing bodywork and skin treatments, but many show up just to sip quality teas from Chinese clay pots in this resplendent Mecca of peace, water, stone and roses.

relax

Tea offerings include aromatic jasmine pearl green tea, organic Lu Shan green tea, various oolong and white teas and a handful of herbal elixirs. Tea Garden Springs welcomes anyone to come enjoy a book, jot a poem, or simply curl up with a couple of almond cookies and a small pot of tea to admire the views of Mount Tamalpais and Mill Valley's charming downtown.

While you are here, you may as well indulge in an Eastern massage or perhaps a "Zen Spa Retreat," which takes four hours and includes either Ayurvedic or aromatherapy massage, a facial and a light meal. If you are lucky enough to be in love, you and your honey can enjoy an intimate bubble bath and simultaneous massages in either the sumptuous Zen Garden Suite or Heaven's Door Suite. Check their website for upcoming tea gatherings and tea classes.

FAR LEAVES TEA

2979 College Avenue
Berkeley, Ca 94705
510.665.9409 | www.farleaves.com
Hours: Daily, 11 a.m. to 9 p.m.

WHEN DONNA LO CHRISTY opened Far Leaves Tea in Berkeley in 1998, fine tea was in the purview of the affluent because of its expense and the erudition that surrounded it. Breaking elitist social patterns became Donna's mission as she set out to provide an affordable but high-quality tea experience for people from all walks of life.

Donna's sincere humility only emphasizes her knowledge of tea. As she unceremoniously pours hot water from pot to porcelain cup, she teaches me how to engage in Chinese tea presentation. "Making tea is a process of meditation. If you pay attention, you can clean your mind. In order to pay attention, you also have to slow down."

She teaches me how to twirl the cylindrical smelling cup back and forth between the palms of my hands, and before turning it over into a small, round sipping cup, we judge the fragrance with

equanimity

slow down

steep

clean mind

adjectives such as "floral," "fruity," "sweet," "creamy," "thick," "acidic," "smooth" and "subtle." As with wines, teas are judged first by their aroma and then by their taste. We place the sipping cups over the smelling cups, hold tight, and then flip them over. Lifting the smelling cup, the tea is ready for tasting.

"The Chinese symbol for drinking is three mouths," Donna says, "which reminds you to taste tea in three steps: first, paying attention to the tip of the tongue to judge sweetness; then to the middle of the tongue for tartness; and finally to the back of the tongue for bitterness."

"I want the tea to be part of your life," she adds. "It's a simple thing to do and you can benefit from it so much."

TEANCE

1780 Fourth Street | Berkeley, Ca 94710
510.524.2832 | www.teance.com
Hours: Sun – Thur, 10 a.m. to 7 p.m.;
Fri & Sat, 10 a.m. to 10 p.m.

TEANCE, LOCATED IN BERKELEY'S EXCLUSIVE Fourth Street shopping district, offers classical Chinese tea culture in a contemporary setting. The bold signature tea bar, made of polished concrete and designed by Fu-Tung Cheng, is embedded with fossils, precious gems, Australian jade and shards of porcelain teacups. This circular, waist-level tea bar harkens back to the Chinese tradition of sipping tea at a round table to encourage the realization of eternity and community without hierarchy. If not in Berkeley, where?

Years back, owner Winnie Yu and friends decided there wasn't a good spot in the Bay Area to meet for quality tea and nowhere to become educated about tea, so they created the kind of stylish meeting place they themselves would want to visit in order to live "the good life" of community, intellectual and spiritual pursuits, and outstanding tea.

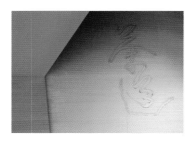

Tea aficionados, as well as those new to exploring tea, will greatly appreciate the care and integrity that infuse this community hub for tea tasting and education. All 65 premium, whole-leaf teas are purchased directly from their places of origin and rotate seasonally. You might think you're at a winery when you receive your menu of "tasting flights" designed for beginner, intermediate and connoisseur-level tea drinkers, with suggested pairings for such treats as finely handcrafted Charles chocolates or Japanese sweets including red-bean mochi.

Teance is also host to a tea connoisseur's group — peopled with filmmakers, artists, Zen monks and probably a few prophets — which meets every Thursday at 5 p.m. In addition, the very popular Young Connoisseur's Club, for kids aged 8-17, meets every other Thursday evening to taste teas, nibble cookies and socialize. Teance offers a fascinating tea experience. Bring your thinking cap and some ready taste buds.

the way to tea

POLENG LOUNGE

1751 Fulton Street | San Francisco, Ca 94117
415.441.1710 | www.polenglounge.com
Hours: Tues – Sun, 4 p.m to 2 a.m.
(10 p.m. to 2 a.m. 21 & over only)

OUR EVER-AMUSING BAY AREA TEA PEOPLE seem able to think of everything. Poleng Lounge in San Francisco has decidedly filled the experimental tea nightclub slot, featuring more than twenty black, oolong, white and green teas, and a number of tea-infused mixed drinks for those who throw traditional tea culture caution to the wind.

Poleng is the Balinese word for duality and perfectly describes what you will experience here: a cocktail bar covered with tea-filled window-box tins that invite customer curiosity to the varied textures, colors, and kinds of teas on order; soft Balinese-style interior design that creates intimacy in a space that holds about 300 people; a "weeping" limestone wall, whose quiet gurgle can be heard close up, but is only seen from a distance when the DJ starts to spin the music; rustic iron teapots with large, contemporary triple hourglass timers to teach customers that different teas require different steeping times; and Chef Timothy Luym's sophisticated culinary creations derived from the fare found in Asian street-hawker food stalls.

It was co-owner/Tea Bacchus Desi Danganan's epiphany while trekking the Inca Trail to Machu Pichu that inspired him to bring tea culture to a new generation of Americans via Poleng Lounge. He observed that whenever tea reaches a new continent, tea culture changes form. If the British could put bergamot in the black tea, maybe he could put green tea in a mixed drink. Before you tea purists wrinkle your noses, I challenge you to try the *Asian Passion Mojito* (mint and lime fused with passion fruit, Bacardi rum, and a dash of green tea). You might just find yourselves raising your glass to toast the new tea generation.

funkadelic

tea bacchus
duality

hip
hop

GREEN GULCH ZEN CENTER

1601 Shoreline Highway
Muir Beach, Ca 94965
415.383.3134
sfzc.org/ggfindex.htm
Hours: By appointment
or public tea gathering

GREEN GULCH FARM and Zen Center — located in a valley halfway between Mill Valley and Muir Beach — has been around for decades. Less well-known is the center's own Sowing the Moon Teahouse, which features a lovely Japanese tea garden that has been nursed to mature beauty by monks at the center.

"The tearoom is a laboratory for studying the self and our relationship with others," says Meiya Wender, whose assignment as Head of Practice at Green Gulch is to oversee the meditation of resident monks as well as the activities of the teahouse. "Soto Zen emphasizes practicing not only in a meditation hall but bringing awareness to all aspects of life. The tearoom supports that kind of attention," she says.

green gulch zen center

The Way of Tea (*Chado*) practiced at this teahouse invites both heightened focus and relaxation as the hostess whips green tea powder (*matcha*) into a froth with her bamboo whisk. The grassy smell of tatami mats and the soft breezes passing through the shoji screens from the nearby Pacific Ocean, provide ample material for rapture and mindfulness. In fact, Japanese Zen monks were responsible for introducing tea to Japan, having learned from Chinese monks that a powerful alertness could replace sleepiness during meditation, after drinking green tea.

To join in a public tea ceremony at Sowing the Moon Teahouse, check the center's website at sfzc.org/ggfindex.htm and then scroll down to click on "teahouse." These public gatherings are held once a month, but not on a regular schedule. Tea ceremony instruction is also provided throughout the year.

TAL-Y-TARA
POLO & TEA SHOPPE

6439 California Street
San Francisco, Ca 94121
415.751.9275
www.talytara.com
Hours: Mon – Sat, noon to 7 p.m.

TEDDY ROOSEVELT ONCE SAID "The outside of a horse is the best thing for the inside of a man." Add tea to that prescription and it would be the perfect motto for Hugh and Melba Meakin, owners of Tal-Y-Tara. In the early 1990s, after losing the lease to their equestrian goods shop, they decided to try running the business from their home. When customers came to buy boots, riding hats and halters, these superb hosts offered British tea with the English riding gear, and their buyers would stay for hours in a caffeinated chat trance.

More than fifteen years later, Tal-Y-Tara Polo and Tea Shoppe continues to combine the love of horses with the love of tea to the delight of Bay Area equestrians. The front retail store sells fabulous English riding gear, as well as casual jackets and sweaters that work as well in a tearoom as they do on the polo field. The back of the shop features a lounge with a few tables and a comfy couch, surrounded by vintage horse-and-rider photos and antique porcelain.

On a sunny day, walk to the rear till you reach the quiet outdoor garden fur-nished with wrought iron chairs and tables, brightened by the surrounding yellow-orange flowers of datura trees.

Try the scones and lemon curd or the tea shop's famous motorloaf — a dark walnut bread, hollowed out to make a variety of tea sandwiches which are then wrapped in waxed paper and reinserted into the bread frame. Ironically, this recipe originated at the turn of the 20th century in New England to feed the "smart set" of early motorcar picnickers who traded in their horses for the first automobiles. I say "Giddyup," anyway.

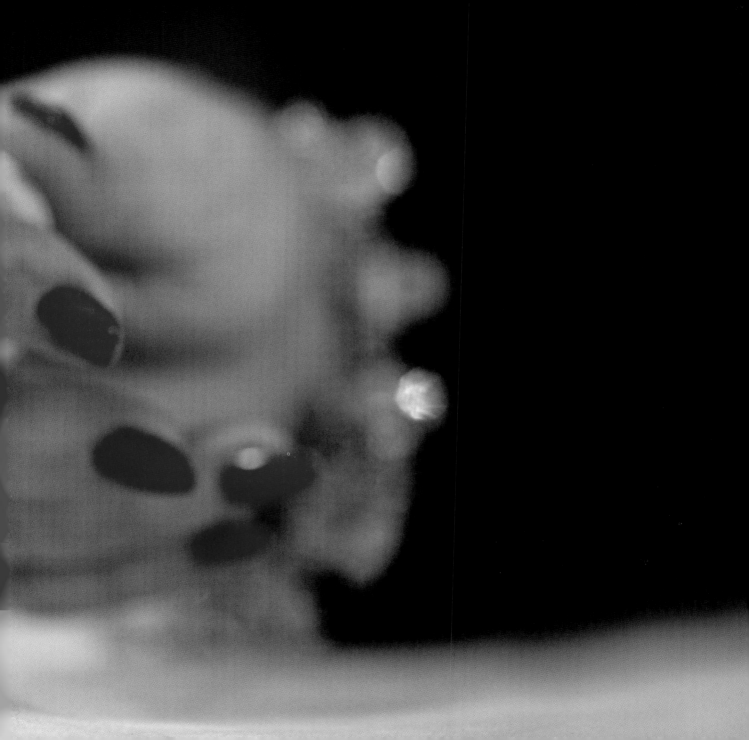

venues   **PART THREE**

SECRET GARDEN

LELAND'S

MODERN TEA

DYNASTEA

LOVEJOY'S

VITAL TEALEAF

fairies

bone china

dress-up

sisters

SECRET GARDEN TEA HOUSE

721 Lincoln Way | San Francisco, Ca 94122
415.566.8834 | www.secretgardenteahouse.net
Hours: Tues – Fri, noon to 6 p.m.; Sat & Sun,
11:30 a.m. to 5:30 p.m.; Closed on Mon and
the first Tues of every month

SISTERS ANNIE AND JANUS LEUNG have created a fairy book tea setting in San Francisco's Inner Sunset district, just opposite Golden Gate Park on Lincoln at Ninth Avenue. From the Royal Albert bone china to the gingham and rose fabric tablecloths and silver place settings, not a detail has been spared in the creation of a fantasy afternoon tea.

Little girls and grown women alike enjoy playing dress-up with the fancy hats, sparkly shoes and fluff-ball wands, as well as being surprised by the little plastic garden fairies that peek out from seemingly nowhere, offering the magic of their unexpected presence. Don't be surprised to find a fair number of men also joining in the fun. Dainty chandeliers sparkle above the intimate dining area where parties for two to twenty-five tea-totallers gather for any remotely feminine occasion or for birthday parties, baby or bridal showers or weekend luxury play dates for kids or grown-ups.

You would be challenged to find better scones anywhere in the Bay Area, and the English tea is precisely prepared. Five different afternoon courses are served,

You would be challenged to find better scones anywhere in the Bay Area, and the English tea is precisely prepared. Five different afternoon courses are served, featuring delicious sandwiches, scones and cream and mini-pastries. One tea service is geared toward 12-and-younger "princes and princesses." Tea sandwiches change seasonally. A small cottage in the rear with its own small kitchen is ideal for large parties and has it's own entrance..

The sisters love to create an atmosphere and mood to inspire enjoyment, friendship and joviality. This is probably the girliest tea party you'll find. Feel free to bring your own garden hat.

the way to tea

LELAND TEA COMPANY

1416 Bush Street
San Francisco, CA 94109
415.346.4832 | www.lelandtea.com
Hours: Daily, 10 a.m. to 7 p.m.

THIS MOM-AND-SON TEAM brings Marilyn Monroe to your table and Cary Grant to the door. Will Otero and Carmen Ortiz run Leland's, where paintings of glamorous characters cover nearly every flat surface, including the wall of the ladies restroom (Guys, you'll have to check the men's room yourselves). This cozy, offbeat setting fuses art deco design and Victorian-flat comfort with Asian rustic nuance. You'll have to see it to believe how well it all works together.

Leland's offers a nice selection of pure and house-blended black, white, green and pu-erh teas, as well as a good number of herbal infusions. Owner Will creates his own fragrant tea blends and loves to engage customers in new creations. He seems to have as much fun naming teas as he does blending them. Try his Tiki Tiki Chai, Kookiedoodle or the Ginger Bolero pu-erh tea.

Mom, a.k.a. Carmen, bakes homemade madeleines on site. One taste of these delicate dreams hot out of the oven will spoil your taste for any other tea cookie. The tea sandwiches are also made by Mom with love and care to the great satisfaction of her adoring customers. For this and many other reasons, Leland's attracts a very loyal following, who seem to stake out a corner table where they can sip tea and chat with a friend or, thanks to free wi-fi access, work at their home-away-from-home office for a couple of hours. This is as good a place to make friends as to bring them. Will even created a spontaneous party for a woman who was new to the Bay Area and who otherwise would have spent her birthday on her own. From this story alone, Will and Carmen deserve the official stamp of the "Real Tea Deal," because friendship and community lie at the heart of the spirit of tea.

Kookiedoodle

home cooking

madeleines

family

art deco

MODERN TEA

602 Hayes Street | San Francisco, Ca 94102
415.626.5406 | www.moderntea.com
Hours: Tue – Fri, 11:30 a.m to 9 p.m;
Sat, 10:30 a.m. to 9 p.m.; Sun, 10:30 a.m. to 6 p.m.

FOR MODERN TEA EXECUTIVE CHEF Alice Cravens, the Bay Area is new and uncharted territory, where an emerging tea culture is just beginning to blossom in the hands of a few committed and capable tea lovers. Alice's vision for Modern Tea echoes the progressive Bay Area values many of us pick up if we are here long enough or are simply paying attention. At Modern Tea you will be served organic, fair-trade, seasonally rotating teas in a light-filled, airy and comfortable restaurant that feels like part summer-camp dining hall and part contemporary art museum. Wooden benches and long tables are matched by solid oak floors, and the elegant copper tea bar is a great place to let Alice pour you a cup of tea or to enjoy a light meal.

The goal at Modern Tea is to provide environmentally sound sourcing of teas, which are economically and intellectually accessible and, at the same time, thoroughly enjoyable. Think and drink up! If you drink up, you might wake up. Something along those lines.

Regardless, if you want to learn about tea or tea history, go straight to Alice. She'll serve you a fascinating flight of teas paired with a delicious salad or an interesting soup such as Chicken Quinoa Chowder. If you arrive in time for Sunday brunch, you can try a plate of waffles made with an 18th century waffle iron. Yummmmm.

the way to tea

DYNASTEA CLUB

1389 Pacific Avenue
San Francisco, Ca 94109
415.931.8620 | www.dynasteaclub.com
Hours: By appointment; check website for
classes and seminars

ACCORDING TO DYNASTEA FOUNDER May Hung, tea drinking is "about reconnecting with nature and reminding ourselves of our relatively small role in a much bigger story." Amen, sister. May feels the calling to spread the true meaning of tea, and as a 74th descendent of Confucius, she's probably just the right person to do this. Licensed in China as a national tea examiner, she is the go-to tea maven for arcane questions about all things *Camellia sinensis*.

Although May recently closed her retail tearoom, she has moved her base of operations just across the street in Russian Hill and is expanding her focus on education and private consultation.

Go to the Dynastea website to find more information on seminars, tea classes, formal Chinese tea ceremony or to buy specialty and wholesale teas. You might also want to indulge in Dynastea's gorgeously designed glassware products to heighten your tea experience.

Like many other "tea people" in the Bay Area, May believes that the value of one's tea experience depends on exercising the qualities of patience, humility and purity in the making and drinking of tea. Tea is an invitation to slow down, connect with yourself, the teapot, the guest and, of course, the tea. "Tea is complex and diverse," says May. "But at the core is simplicity and purity."

purity

patience

confucius

tang

immortal

the way to tea

LOVEJOY'S TEA ROOM

1351 Church Street
San Francisco, Ca 94114
415.648.5895
www.lovejoystearoom.com
Hours: Wed – Sun, 11 a.m. to 6 p.m.

AS ONE CUSTOMER PUT IT, "Lovejoy's is just like home, only without all the baggage." Somehow tearooms like this one create an atmosphere of suspend-ed animation and judgment that allows for a heightened sense of intimacy and sharing between friends, lovers or even complete strangers. But there is no other tearoom like Lovejoy's, which must account for the three-week wait for a week-end reservation.

Lovejoy's also doubles as an antique store, so if you find yourself endeared to the teapot, its mismatched teacup or even the chair you're sitting on, you can buy it. Have you fallen in love with the antique tea tower that keeps your scones and finger sandwiches so nicely aloft? It's yours for the buying.

This very comfy, informal tearoom is the brainchild of Muna Nash and Gillian Briley, who work tirelessly to provide an atmosphere of fun and relaxation and offer the romantic luxury of a British afternoon tea. Old sofas are lovingly adorned

old lace

tea tower

kinship

petits fours

vintage

with vintage lace, and cheerful servers *swooosh* through the place with tea trays overflowing with the most scrumptious finger sandwiches, scones, salads, crumpets, fruit and all the sweet condiments you could hope for. Black, green and black flavored teas as well as herbal tisanes are served. Extra special menu items include pasties, shepherd's pie and a "Ploughman's Lunch" featuring cheeses, salads and toast points. Prices are more than reasonable.

Across the street you will find Lovejoy's antique store, which packs in the overflow items that have burst the seams of the tearoom. An afternoon of tea and antiques is sure to bring out the bloom on any loved-one's cheek. May as well leave even your carry-on baggage at home.

VITAL TEALEAF

1044 Grant Avenue
San Francisco, CA 94133
415.981.2388
www.vitaltleaf.com
Hours: Daily, 10 a.m. to 8 p.m.

VITAL TEALEAF WILL ALWAYS BE MY first tea love. Before Uncle Gee invited me in from Grant Street for a tasting, I assumed there was nothing more to tea than Earl Grey and English Breakfast. *Au contraire*. With more than 350 varieties, Vital Tealeaf is a perfect starting place for tasting and learning about tea. While sipping the incomparable tang of Seven Monks One Lady or reveling in the

furling steam of Supreme Water Fairy, one gets a sense of the challenges and nuances that a "simple" cup of tea can present and why tea is becoming such a big deal in the culinary world. The colors, textures and lively fragrances of the large assortment of teas at Vital Tealeaf make for a sensual feast.

Answering questions such as what teas to serve with a seafood brunch or how to get over your chronic indigestion, daily stress or skin condition, proprietor Ming Duong and his gregarious staff will gladly pour you a half-dozen different teas and make recommendations, from the graceful and culinary, to the spiritual and medicinal, to the more theatrically personal ("If your boyfriend ever dishonors you, tell him you know Uncle Gee, and that I will take care of him!") How fun is that?

Vital Tealeaf is a particularly great spot to bring kids because tea preparation is a vivid and charming presentation here, especially when they drop a ball of tea into a wineglass to see it bloom into a greenish-yellow flower with a bright red center. You will leave Vital Tealeaf with new friends, knowledge, joy and of course, a bag of exquisite tea. As Uncle Gee says, "You arrive here as a stranger; when you leave, you are a part of my family."

the way to tea

a few thoughts
for the pot

WATER

Making a great cup of tea begins with using the best water available. In *The Classic of Tea*, Lu Yu specified which types of water to use or avoid:

"Water from slow-flowing streams, the stone-lined pools or milk-pure springs is the best of mountain water. Never take tea made from water that falls in cascades, gushes from springs, rushes in a torrent or that eddies and surges as if nature were rinsing its mouth."

While we, unfortunately, can no longer collect water from our neighborhood springs to brew a pot of tea, we can consider the quality of water available to us and do whatever possible to encourage our local, regional and national leaders to work towards ensuring clean, toxin-free water, not only for the sake of a clean cup of tea, but for the health of our families and community. If not us, who? If not now, when?

ORGANICS

You wouldn't think of adding a few drops of Deet to sweeten the teapot, so why buy teas sprayed with pesticides? Selecting organically grown teas sends a message to tea sellers and growers that you want wholesome products and that you care about the health of our planet — from your family to the plants, soil and streams to the folks around the globe who pick, harvest and process teas.

FAIR TRADE

Ask your local tea seller about fair trade practices, which protect the rights and incomes of our overseas friends who provide us with great tea. Let our good fortune of imbibing in tea be their good fortune also. All for one, and one for all. Let's not only toast to it but act on it.

tea:

the inside scoop

THERE ARE MORE THAN 300,000 different teas in the world, so even a tea zealot will be kept busy exploring tea for a lifetime. This is what makes tea so engaging and so much fun. Like wine, each tea has its own characteristics and disposition. Even more interestingly, that character is influenced by the water used in tea preparation, the person brewing the tea and the pot in which it is brewed. So each time a tea is brewed, it can and will manifest a nuanced variation. In fact, the skill level of the server of traditional Chinese tea presentation is determined by his or her ability to make three different tasting teas from one serving of leaves.

Tea is defined as an infusion of any variety of the *Camellia sinensis* bush or tree, which is indigenous to China and India, but has found its way to many locations around the world, most particularly in Asia. There are three primary tea types: black, green and oolong; but most tea aficionados include two more distinctive categories: white tea, which is a subcategory of green tea; and pu-erh tea, the base of which can be black or green tea, but is processed in distinctive ways.

TEA TYPES ARE FURTHER DISTINGUISHED BY SEVERAL CRITERIA

Variety: There are several botanical varieties of each of the main tea types. Tea aficionados judge tea in much the same way that wine lovers judge wine grapes. There are approximately 2500 distinctive varieties of the *Camellia sinensis* plant. Bilo Chun and Dragonwell are examples of varieties of green tea.

Harvest Season: First-harvest teas are usually considered to be of a higher quality than subsequent harvests. The first harvest generally

takes place in the spring season, but can take place during other seasons, depending on the variety of tea and where it's grown.

Location and Terroir: Different varieties of teas can be grown in several geographic locations and conditions, which will influence the characteristics of each tea. Certain varieties are indigenous to particular areas of Asia, and for tea purists, teas grown in the place of origin are superior to those that are transplanted to other regions. *Terroir* is a French term meaning "of the earth," and is most familiarly used with respect to the growing of wine grapes. Soil type, surrounding flora, altitude, climatic conditions and even which side of the mountain a tea plant is grown on will describe the *terroir* of the tea and will influence the tea's final expression. If there are jasmine bushes in the area where the tea is being grown, for example, the scent of the jasmine will influence the tea's character, and a tea specialist will appreciate this distinction.

Crafting: Crafting refers to everything that involves processing fresh leaves and turning those leaves into a finished tea. We in the West are used to mass processing of foods and beverages and, in contrast, the processing of teas is often delightfully intimate; many of them are picked by hand and processed by an individual with various natural objects like bamboo, wood boxes, woks and special racks. Aspects of crafting include the following:

- Degree of Oxidation: Tea is not fermented, but oxidized. When tea is exposed to air (or oxygen), a number of natural chemical reactions occur and this process is called oxidation. Enzymatic oxidation is caused by polyphenol oxidase, an enzyme that is present in the tea leaf (and in most plants for that matter). Once exposed to oxygen, the enzyme converts the catechins in the leaves into red and brown compounds and flavonoids that give black tea its color and flavor. Any sort of heat (steaming, roasting, firing, etc.) stops the enzymatic breakdown. The time for which teas are allowed to oxidize determines the richness or subtlety of the tea as well as its color. Tea connoisseurs describe the *liquor* of the teas for their color and character, which is largely influenced by whether, how and for how long the tea has been exposed to the air. Many teas are oxidized by being laid on special racks made of local woods or bamboos by the farmers themselves.

- Firing: All teas are either steamed or fired. This is what arrests the oxidation process, and firing also decreases moisture content in the leaves. The method of heating and firing contributes to the flavor profile of the tea. Some teas, for example, are pan-fired on a wok or on iron pans.

- Roasting: This part of the process dries and twists the tea leaves.

- Rolling: Tea can be rolled by hand or by machine.

Rolling breaks the cell walls of the leaves and activates the polyphenols responsible for tea's antioxidant activity, which reputedly offers so many health benefits.

- Scenting: Proper scenting of teas involves laying flower blossoms, fruit rind or other fragrant substances onto the leaves, sometimes in several sessions, and then removing them. Teas are also sometimes scented with oils, as in Earl Grey which is scented with bergamot oil. Tea connoisseurs tend to favor the former method of scenting, particularly when the tea is scented with the blossoms of plants or trees growing in the immediate vicinity of the tea plants.

- Preparation: The final fragrance and taste of a tea depends a lot on how it's made. Whether you are brewing a pot of English tea or traditional Indian Chai tea, engaging in Chinese *Gong fu* presentation or aspiring to develop your skill as a practitioner of Japanese tea ceremony, you will have plenty to concentrate on. A visit to Eastern Europe, the Middle East, South America, Tibet, Turkey or any number of other countries or regions will teach you myriad variations of the science and etiquette of tea preparation. What fun to explore tea — and the world — with the goal of learning more about tea and its many names and expressions.

- Note: Many tea enthusiasts favor using loose-leaf teas, regardless of the intended method of preparation.

basic tea glossary

THE FIVE MAIN TEA TYPES are black, green, oolong, white, and pu-erh. Herbal infusions are included as a service to the many folks who enjoy sipping hot brewed flowers, leaves and roots of other plants besides *Camellia sinensis.* It is important to note that plant infusions made with anything other than *Camellia sinensis* are not considered to be teas but are referred to as infusions or tisanes.

Black Teas are fully oxidized after having been withered, twisted, and rolled. The oxidation process changes the leaves' color from green to a deep reddish brown or amber (which is why Chinese call it *red* tea). Black teas offer a robust flavor that is rich and complex.

Most popular black teas consumed in the West — like Earl Grey or English and Irish Breakfast teas — are blended teas that arrive in the cup in prepared teabags. They generally contain some combination of Assam, Keemun or Ceylon teas. Milk, sugar and/or lemon are often added before serving. In contrast, Chinese tend to be purists, serving loose-leaf, single-variety, black teas like Lapsang Souchong and Dian Hong, and black teas tend to be consumed without condiments. In India, you will see young children in the streets with their pots and pans over charcoal or wood fires not far from their large white cows that provide milk for the black-tea-based *Chai,* which is made with low-grade black teas boiled in milk and infused with lots of sugar and spices like cardamon, cloves and pepper. The major difference between Chinese and Indian/Ceylon (Sri Lankan) teas is varietal. Chinese teas are *Camellia sinensis sinensis,* Indian teas are traditionally *Camellia sinensis assamica,* although as times have changed, Indian teas, namely the pu-erhs grown in Assam, are now found to be more correctly

classified as *Camellia sinensis yunnan*, because they originate from this Chinese varietal.

Black teas are generally brewed with water at boiling temperature or slightly below.

EXAMPLES OF BLACK TEA INCLUDE:
Keemun: A smooth, fragrant, full-bodied Chinese tea, which is often served in the West with milk and sugar or lemon, and by Chinese without condiments.
Lapsang Souchong: This is a dark red Chinese tea that has been smoked on wooden racks over pine fires. A good winter drink, it is often enhanced with milk and sugar. Real Lapsang Souchong is rare and comes from the Wuyi Mountains in the Fujian province of China. Souchong was originally a lower grade oolong that was accidentally smoked by pine needles.
Darjeeling: This black tea hails from the Himalayan foothills of West Bengal in Eastern India. More tea is sold as Darjeeling tea than is produced in Darjeeling, so look for the official seal from the Tea Board of India to be sure you have gotten the real thing.
Ceylon: Sri Lanka is one of the largest tea producing regions in the world. Ceylon teas are often included in blended teas like English or Irish breakfast teas.
Assam: This Indian tea is a widely used black tea, which is often used in blends.
Earl Grey: This black tea is scented with bergamot oil. Its eponymous name is probably apocryphal, as the tea existed before the British landed in Asia.

Green Teas are usually steamed as soon as they are picked so that they do not become oxidized, and then they are later dried with heat. Certain green teas are pan-fired without steaming. Green teas are generally pale green or greenish-gold in color, and are marked by their fresh and subtle flavor. They are considered by many to have the most health benefits of all the tea varieties and often are high in antioxidants yet low in caffeine. Other possible health benefits associated with green tea are lowered cholesterol, cancer fighting properties, fertility enhancement, weight loss and lowered risk of heart attack.

Green teas were first powdered by Chan monks in China, whose traditions later evolved into Zen Buddhist tea ceremony in Japan. Like all teas, green tea is indigenous to China, and Chinese green teas are prepared and cultivated in many different styles, such as rolled, ground, twisted, etc. They are also sometimes scented with flowers like jasmine or rose. The best scented teas are produced

by fresh flower petals being strewn several times on the unprocessed tea, then being removed by hand before further processing.

Harvest season plays a critical role in determining the quality of a green tea. Spring harvest green teas are always the best and highest quality because the leaves are picked when they are still tender. Most supermarket variety green teas and tea bags are late-season, fairly low-grade teas.

Green tea should be brewed in water that is well below boiling temperature, usually for two minutes or less, and often for less than a minute.

EXAMPLES OF GREEN TEA INCLUDE:

Green Snail Spring (Bi Lo Chun): This Chinese green tea can also be grown in Taiwan, but originated in the mountains in Jiangsu Province, China.

Dragon Well (Long Jing): Perhaps the best known green tea in the West, Dragon Well is harvested in the Chinese village of Dragon Well in the mountains of Zhejiang Province, and is considered one of the highest grade teas. It is known for its beautiful jade-green color and orchid-like fragrance.

Yellow Mountain Fur Peak (Huang Shan Mao Feng): This lovely tea has emerald-green leaves and is found in the Anhui Province of China. It has a light and flowery fragrance.

Sencha: A roasted Japanese tea, Sencha is steamed before hot-air drying and then pan firing, all as preparation before steeping.

Matcha: This finely powdered green tea is used in Japanese tea ceremony, wherein it is whisked into a light froth in a ceramic bowl and then consumed in the same bowl in which it was prepared.

Oolong Teas are partly oxidized, withered and rolled, and are stronger than green teas, but more delicate than the fully oxidized black teas. The word oolong means black dragon and comes from a folkloric story in which a Chinese farmer gets scared off by a black dragon while picking tea, and during his absence, his tea becomes partly oxidized. Lo and behold, the leaves produced a delicious brew.

Although oolongs are harvested in several Asian countries, the more expensive oolongs are grown exclusively in China and Taiwan, the best of them at higher altitudes. Oolongs are often named after the region or altitude at which they are cultivated. The most popular of these flavorful and aromatic teas are produced primarily in three regions: the Wuyi Mountains of Fujian Province, China, which offer Wuyi oolongs; The Anxi region of Fujian Province; and Taiwan, which produces High Mountain or Formosa oolongs. Tea purists are often drawn to oolongs as they are considered to be the most complex of all the tea types.

Oolongs are often used in Chinese *Gong fu* presentation, done with Yixing red clay pots. The porous pots are made from a rare purple clay found only in Yixing, China, and the pots themselves are greatly treasured intimate objects of the owners, as the oils from the teas and from the server's own fingers enrich and distinguish the teapot and therefore the tea that is made from them.

Like black tea, oolong tea is reputed for its ability to emulsify fat and cholesterol, and so makes a great beverage for anyone inclined towards fried foods. Brewing temperatures vary between 180° to 210°F.

EXAMPLES OF OOLONG TEA INCLUDE:

Iron Goddess (Ti Guan Yin): This Chinese tea refers to the healing powers of the female Buddhist goddess of compassion, Guan Yin. The tea's name connotes its robust but smooth flavor and legendary power to heal even a Chinese emperor.

Water Fairy (Shui Xian): This Wuyi oolong is known for its spectacular fragrance. The dark green leaves produce a sweet liquor. It originates in Wuyi Province, China.

Profound Orchid (Wuyi Qi Lan): This Wuyi oolong is known for its sweet, floral flavor. It is grown in the cliffs of the Wuyi Mountians, which is the original home of oolongs.

Phoenix Mountain Honey Dan Chong (Feng Huang Mi Xian Dan Chong): This tea comes from one of the most important areas of southern China where oolongs originate.

Iron Warrior Monk (Tie Luo Han): The name refers to buddhist monks engaged in the mind strengthening practice of martial arts, and who historically tend to the tea bushes in the Wuyi Mountains.

Frozen Summit Mountain (Dong Ding): This very popular tea is named for the way in which the tea is specially crafted by artisans in Nantou, Taiwan. The tea is also grown and harvested outside of Lugu region of Nantou, where it originates. It's known to possess a smooth, rich and fruity taste.

White Teas are really a subset of green tea, but are distinguished by having been picked prior to reaching full maturity, before the buds have opened. This makes the flavor of white teas even milder than green teas and produces a light gold or pale yellow liquor. Only the tips or buds of the tea plant are processed. Simple processing includes steaming and drying. Produced exclusively in China, they are very highly prized for their light, fragrant brews, high antioxidant count and low caffeine.

White teas tend to be sipped without a meal as their subtlety requires a clean palate and full attention to detail. They were previously available only from the best specialty tea stores and importers, but now can be found on the shelves of high-end grocery stores. We can only hope that the popularity of these teas will not result in a compromise of their quality, as large commercial importers poise themselves to mass produce and package them. *Caveat emptor!* Better yet, buy from your local specialty tea store, where the seller will probably know the tea farmer.

EXAMPLES OF WHITE TEA INCLUDE:
Silver Needle (Bai Hau Yin Zhen): Silver needle is one of the highest-grade and most popular white teas. The buds only are harvested during just a few choice days in early spring. As its name suggests, the tea buds are covered with fine silvery hairs. It has a subtle, flowery and fruity bouquet.

Noble Longlife Eyebrow (Shou Mei): This heartier white tea is a late-harvest pick and the tips and leaves are shaped like eyebrows.

White Peony (Bai Mu Dan): This classic white tea is sometimes also called "longevity eyebrows" for its rust colored leaves and buds. It is generally covered with fine silvery-white hairs.

Snow Buds (Xue Ya): A rare white tea covered in silvery down, this tea is hand harvested in Fujian Province of China. It has a grain-like flavor that is both sweet and savory.

Ceylon White: Sri Lanka too produces a popular white tea that is used in many prepackaged teas more often found in supermarkets than in specialty stores.

Pu-erh Teas are actually black and green teas, but they are so uniquely processed as to necessitate a category unto themselves. They are large-leaf teas named for the tea trading center in Yunnan, China, from where they originate. There are two basic types of pu-erh teas, one which comes from a fully oxidized dark black tea and one which is only partly oxidized. They can be sold as loose-leaf teas or in compressed cakes, disks, bowls, bricks or even in bamboo tubes.

They are not only some of the most traditional teas in China, they are also sometimes the most esoteric and intriguing, especially for tea enthusiasts. Once used as real currency in China, pu-erhs increase in value as they age over decades. Some "collectors" in the Bay Area have decided that sitting on pu-erhs might be a better bet than banking on mutual funds. Incidentally, the damp, cool, foggy climate of the Bay Area happens to be an excellent place for these teas to age. The best pu-erhs are picked in spring and autumn. Their earthy fragrances vary from the "dirt tea" reputation given them by some Westerners, to the elegant, mysterious gaian aromas they can present. The Chinese commonly use pu-erhs to combat indigestion. Caffeine levels vary greatly.

EXAMPLES OF PU-ERH TEA INCLUDE:

Tuo Cha: These compressed, bowl-shaped cakes are often wrapped in pretty Chinese paper and can make a fun gift. Their earthy taste is rich and unmistakable.

Tibetan Pu-erh: Grown and processed in China, Tibetan pu-erh is often shaped like a mushroom and is used as both food and tea by Tibetans who shave off pieces of the teacakes and mix them with yak butter for a calorie-laden and filling snack.

Lu An: This age-old country blend has a dirt-like aroma, due to the exposure of the leaves to moisture. As with most pu-erhs, the method for aging the tea is top secret.

Jade Pu-erh: Jade pu-erhs are compressed green teas that are noted for their full-bodied, smooth finish.

Herbal Infusions or Tisanes are not considered by purists to be teas at all as they come from a variety of plants and not from the *Camellia sinensis* plant. You can brew any digestible plant or spice for a medicinal or tasty infusion, but don't call it tea if you are within shouting range of a true tea fanatic.

EXAMPLES OF TISANES INCLUDE:

Chamomile: Steep golden flowers from the chamomile plant to relax your nerves and get ready to settle down to sleep.

Peppermint: Peppermint leaves love to take up a big patch in the garden and taste great as hot or cold infusions.

Chrysanthemum: Flowers from the chrysanthemum plant make a great brew for detoxification and for a cooling effect. They are also often blended with "real" teas.

Rooiboos: Infusions from this African red bush plant have become the rage for the plant's healing reputation and its tea-like taste. Vanilla rooiboos is a piece of heaven, but, alas, it's not tea.

Rose: What could be more romantic and soothing than an infusion of rose buds or petals? This delicate flower infusion is the nectar of goddesses, especially those who value soft, clear skin.

tea for health and vitality

are not often motivated by political or religious concerns to exchange their coffee mugs or wine glasses for tea cups. Instead, as they add up the many demerits of coffee or alcohol and compare this to the huge number of health perks offered by tea, they can't help choosing tea. While coffee or alcohol are variously rumored to contribute to skin problems, ulcers, reproductive health risks, heart ailments and anxiety, tea is reportedly inclined to alleviate, or at least not cause, these maladies.

Chinese and Japanese tea drinkers have relied on the healing support of tea for centuries, and European folk wisdom has also encouraged the use of a cup of tea to ease nervous tension and other ailments. Yet Western science is only now catching up, providing statistically significant documentation that nods to commonly held beliefs. Just as some Tibetan lamas and other mystics respond to the scientific findings of subatomic physicists with a "Well, yeah, we've known that for a few thousand years — what else did you expect?" the Chinese can sit back with satisfied grins as one research paper after another comes to the public with new "discoveries" regarding tea's possible health benefits.

To begin with, tea contains an abundance of antioxidants called polyphenols. Much attention has been given to the role of antioxidants in halting free radical damage in our cells, which is a byproduct of the oxidation process. When our cells oxidize, they send off free radicals, which damages DNA and cell membranes. In turn, this process can lead to heart disease, certain kinds of cancer, stroke and other afflications. Tea sippers and researchers believe tea's strong antioxidants may help prolong life and protect the human body from disease. Supposedly much of the antioxidant action comes from flavonoids, and tea is one of the most highly flavonoid-laden plants on earth.

Tea also has great nutritional value, as acknowledged by the many people in Asia for whom tea is a food as well as a beverage. Tea contains vitamins B6, B12, C, K and E and a host of amino acids, including one of great interest to scientists, L-theanine. L-theanine was tested by researchers at Brigham and Women's Hospital and showed statistically significant results in assisting immune system response, from resisting bacteria and viruses to leavening one's mental outlook. Go Tea!

Despite the fact that all teas originate from the same plant — *Camellia sinensis* — they are grown and processed very differently (see *The Inside Scoop*). As such they have different properties, different vitamin and antioxidant profiles and varying levels of caffeine. (*Anyone with a serious physical or psychological health concern would want to check with a doctor, herbalist, or naturopath before drinking tea, which can be highly or lightly — but always — caffeinated.*) The addition of condiments is also sometimes said to dispel the health benefits made available by a cup of tea in the first place. So, do your homework, folks, before adding milk or sipping a "mok-12"-caffeine tea.

All the facts on tea's health benefits are not in, and, of course, scientists seem to gain great pleasure in disagreeing with each other, so sleuthing out the eternal truth of tea's corporeal benefits is for those who love a mission. If you take a moment out of your day to research the health benefits of tea online or at the library, you will find a multitude of books and other references to lead you forward.

Here's to your health and happiness with every sip you take!

The Classic of Tea *By Lu Yu*

New Tea Lover's Treasury: The Classic True Story of Tea
By James Norwood Pratt

All the Tea in China *By Kit Chow & Ione Kramer*

The Green Tea User's Manual *By Helen Gustafson*

The New Tea Companion: A Guide to Teas Throughout the World
By Jane Pettigrew and Bruce Richardson

The Way of Tea *By Master Lam Km Chuen and Lam Kai Sin*

The Book of Tea *By Kakuzo Okakura*

The Book of Tea *By Alain Stella, Gilles Brochard, Nadine Beautheac,
Catherine Dozel and Marc Walter*

The Time of Tea *By Dominique Pasqualini & Bruno Suet*

ACKNOWLEDGMENTS   *To family, friends, mentors and colleagues*

SO MANY PEOPLE HAD A HAND in creating this book. Somehow tea brings out our sense of connectedness and the higher instinct to share what is best in us. I am grateful to so many people who have given this project their very best.

First, without the great integrity, wisdom, kindness and enthusiasm of all the "tea people" who have created fabulous venues for us to learn about and enjoy tea, this book would not exist. They have enriched our community and worked tirelessly to provide us with havens for fun, relaxation, intellectual stimulation, spiritual practice, serenity and great tea! Also, many people allowed me the honor of photographing them while they sipped tea with their friends and family. I hope the click of the shutter added to the amusement of their tea experience.

Muna Nash of Lovejoy's gave me the first idea for this book. Sandra Eisert's keen and caring wisdom and support gave the book what it needed to grow and become real. Editor John Orr tempered the lunacy that is born of late-night writing and kept me on the straight and narrow word by word. Mark Rutherford's outstanding skill at preparing images for press deserves high praise. Peter Dombrowski offered substantial knowledge of publishing — as well as kindness and integrity — at critical moments. Kirk Paulsen and the Aperture team at Apple Inc. provided me with the tools to produce this book with grace and agility. Thanks to Chuck Goldhaber at Far Leaves Tea in Berkeley for helping me with first ideas about Tea:

The Inside Scoop, and to Peter Luong at Red Blossom Tea Company and Winnie Yu at Teance for overseeing its accuracy and completion.

Nancy Campana provided the excellence of her design skills to create a foundation for the book, and Birgit Wick, designer extraordinaire, helped to shape the final layout into something meaningful, offering guidance, kindness and as always, the delights of her friendship. Meredith Brejla introduced me to the many fine folks at Earth Aware Editions who graciously shared their support and good cheer.

Special thanks to friends and mentors (some of whom are both) who offered love and laughter, and challenged me to do my best work: Kim Komenich, Jim Sugar, Arthur Blaustein, Ellen Visser, Karyn Sanders, Rina Sircar, Larrain Appelbaum, Dee Mullen, Shelly Davidson, Darold Simms, Karen Johnson and Monica Suder. I also especially want to thank James Norwood Pratt for his kindness, knowledge and generosity.

I offer deep gratitude to my parents, Robert and Grace Sauer — and to my sister and dearest friend, Elissa Whelchel — for their love and constant support; and to Steven Roy Neuner for his love, inspiration and faith in this project. Only with love does any achievement matter.

And finally, a deep bow to Shen Nung and Lu Yu, the original tea saints who shared their knowledge and love of the magical tea plant, *Camellia sinensis*.